Danielle Hanson must be the incarnation of Gaston Bachelard's ideal poet, a poet who acutely observes a world as she makes it new. With a vocabulary of images as diverse as slugs, animals, flowers, constellations and emotions, as well as startling situations, she brings us a surrealistic vision that also reads like a rational explanation. A poem titled "Eating His Dead Wife" gives us one side, a bird eating the reflection of a building gives us another. When she travels, her succinct, epigrammatic descriptions reveal more than most poets can in much longer poems: "The cobblestones were tense and / looking for crumbs. The sea / waiting to devour the sun," she says about Puerto Angel. This is an amazing first book, book I cherish, for every page I turn makes me see the world differently, astoundingly, reverently. It's a book that never ends.

> —Richard Jackson, author of fourteen books of poems, including *Traversings*, with Robert Vivian, *Out of Place* (Ben Franklin Award), and *Resonance* (Eric Hoffer Award).

Danielle Hanson's new book *Ambushing Water* has a deliberate clarity that vibrates through her music and imagery like a crystal glass tapped gently with the bright butter knife. Danielle has always written the most original, provocative yet inevitable love poems. She is simply brilliant.

> —Norman Dubie, international recipient of the 2016 Griffin Poetry Prize and author of twenty-eight collections of poetry, including *The Quotations of Bone*.

So often in this collection, the circumstance in a single poem offers an unlikely though compelling route into intimacy—"eating his dead wife's ashes / in his cereal every morning" for example—until the circumstances build to near breaking and the poems show themselves as a constant, valiant, smart struggle to keep the always-vulnerable speaker above water. So many new words are quietly and easily introduced to the world—earthfish, rainstars, mooncat, slugquistadores, sky-puddles—which seems appropriate in these efforts at finding new places to find purchase, new ways to hold on. The poems repeatedly find that new ground, and as readers we hold on just as firmly as the speaker every time.

> —Alberto Rios, Arizona's first poet laureate and author of ten books and chapbooks of poetry, including *A Small Story about the Sky*, three collections of short stories, and a memoir.

Ambushing Water is compelling in its restraint: lyricism is deepened and amplified in these often short, always indelible poems. Danielle Hanson writes of the mysteries of the natural world: "How laughable is the moon / as an equal sign." This interrogation of worlds, inner and outer, the self and the earth, gives this collection its transformative power and renders everything new and strange and beautiful.

> —Paul Guest, author of four full-length poetry collections, including *My Index of Slightly Horrifying Knowledge*, and a memoir, *One More Theory about Happiness*.

AMBUSHING WATER

AMBUSHING WATER

Poems by Danielle Hanson

BRICK ROAD

POETRY PRESS

Library of Congress Control Number: 2016958093
ISBN-13: 978-0-9979559-0-3

Published by Brick Road Poetry Press
513 Broadway
Columbus, GA 31902-0751
www.brickroadpoetrypress.com

Brick Road logo by Dwight New

For Magnus, Annika, and Olivia

Acknowledgments

Thank you to the editors of the following journals and anthologies in which these poems first appeared, sometimes in an earlier form:

all roads will lead you home: "Astronomy," "Saying Goodbye to the Slugs"

Apple Valley Review: "It's Late Autumn and the Few Leaves Left Clinging to the Trees Beg to Be Pulled Off," "Red Nail Polish"

The Asheville Poetry Review: "After the Tree", "Just a Moment Ago"

Blackbird: "Lemon Breast of the Virgin Mary"

Blood Orange Review: "Puddle Bird"

Burningword Literary Journal: "Burial"

Carriage House Review: "The Killed Bug," "The Statue Licker"

Cimarron Review: "Igneous" (reprinted in *Poets Against the War Anthology*)

Clackamas Literary Review: "Ellijay"

Clapboard House: "Pick-Up at the Dead End Supermarket," "I Have Other Things on My Mind"

The Comstock Review: "The Empty Mailbox"

The Cortland Review: "Lily"

The English Journal: "Picking Blueberries," "Traveling"

Folly: "A Possibility"

Hayden's Ferry Review: "Bird"

Hiram Poetry Review: "Eating His Dead Wife"

Hubbub: "Snake"

Iodine Poetry Journal: "Nightmare"

Lake Effect: A Journal of Literary Arts: "The Man is Walking His Bird on a Leash"

The Lucid Stone: "Saying Goodbye to a Friend"

Mudfish: "Home Sick"

Nebraska Review: "The Break Up," "Horse Tracks"

The Pedestal Magazine: "Elderly Breasts"

Pembroke Magazine: "Outside the Moon"

Pennsylvania Literary Review: "Cat"

Roanoke Review: "The Day the Air Conditioning Broke in the Wax Museum"

Rosebud: "You"

Shout Them From the Mountaintops: Georgia Poems: "Hiking in
Slovenia," "Still"
The Sow's Ear Poetry Review: "In Puerto Angel"
Willow Springs: "The Bird Eats a Building," "Cruel Son," "He Beat
Her"

"Red Nail Polish" was nominated by the editor of *Apple Valley
Review* for a Best of the Net prize in 2011.

"After the Tree" was nominated for a Pushcart Prize by the editor
of *The Asheville Poetry Review* in 2007.

Thank you to the faculties at the University of Tennessee at Chattanooga and Arizona State University for their support and care for my work, especially Richard Jackson, a peerless mentor; Beckian Fritz Goldberg; Norman Dubie; and Alberto Rios. Thank you to my fellow students in both programs for helping form my voice: Bradley Paul, Karri Harrison Paul, Ted Howard, Laurel Snyder, Julia Beach Anderson, Paul Guest, Jennifer Ryan, Victoria Raschke, Caroline Klocksiem, Zeenat Potia, Verania White Hammond . . . . Thank you to Karri Harrison Paul also for the use of her work for the cover art. Love to you all!

Thank you to the editors and staff of the journals who have selected my work, to the Hambidge Center for supporting me during the creation of this work, and to my community in Grant Park for being my creative tribe and home.

A deep and special gratitude to my husband, Magnus Egerstedt, who is an inspiration and careful reader. Thanks to my girls Annika and Olivia, and to my parents Jean and Dan, for their support.

Thank you to the editors of Brick Road Poetry Press for selecting my work to represent their vision. Peace!

Contents

You

The rain wouldn't stop;
it came inside
the mind, like the sound
of canned laughter over music,
like hundreds of chickens
gone crazy
after so many generations.

Bird

The bird is almost touched
by shadow and begins
to close up
like a tulip.
It starts with the wings
pointing straight up at sky,
then tucking under and into her body.
The beak is next,
curling until disappeared.
The head follows,
a slow vortex slowing.
Finally the entire bird
has folded in on herself,
simply dissolved,
leaving nothing but a vague black perfume.
A leaf falls. The whole of night clings to that leaf.

After the Tree

After the tree was felled
it took a week
for its shadow
to leave the root.
Longer still for the shadows of birds—
and so it was,
they hovered mid-ground,
preening, chirping, hopping absurdly
into nothingness.
Cats pounced until bored.
The birds woke with the sun
until fall came. It was months
before the shadows of their songs fell silent.

He Beat Her

And her back fell open
like a moth finding its wings.
He beat her and her back flew
open like a bird rising.
He beat her and her back
flew to a tree—
a tree was sketched
by the markings on her back.
He beat her and her back left
running so hard
it left its feet behind.

Red Nail Polish

You asked me to paint my nails red
and so, of course, I did
even though I hated the way
they stalked the eye.
My hand was suddenly not my own.
It was five cherry bombs
waiting to go off.
My arm was the shadow
of a red light district.

I should have gone but it was too late.
Fire ants were marching,
the sun was red and multiple,
the blue was red, the green, everything.

I wanted to cut my fingers off, escape,
but that would only let the color run
to the counter, the floor,
multiply like cockroaches and hide in the dark.
I couldn't get them all anyway.
What would I do when one hand was only a stub?
I needed them. How could I sever them from you?

Igneous

Tonight the goddess of love and war
is spitting the wind in our direction.
Regardless, you light candles
as if to lose some sun before tomorrow,
as if to hold the past as a smoldering match.
I am watching you hunt for the right words
and not to take you out of context
but someone has to take you
down this river. It's been more times
than I've stood on the shore feeling the earth move,
feeling the mountains being exhumed.
I looked to continental drift theory,
discovered the heat, the radioactive decay,
feeding those peaks of lava,
tearing the ground apart beneath us like a hawk.
I know that I've looked into those chasms and seen you,
that losing you is forgetting love,
that it's the sharpest blade you cannot feel.

Bad Boys

Ever since
the slingshot boys
shattered the streetlight,
darkness has been collecting
bits of itself
into a lonely corner
like a homesick
golem.

After a Nap and Groggy

I have done so little.
Today is aggressive, short.

I've lost something,
forgotten something.

The flies have carried away our dreams
to build nests on cliffs too windy for memory.

They circle overhead like the fan
echoing: Come over. It's late. I am alone.

Into the Air

The trees melted into the air.
—Ezra Pound

The smoke is rising to the trees,
resting before continuing into clouds.
We haven't yet started the flames.
It must be my love for you
waking the sleeping birds
then dissipating as they choke their young.

Is this the end?
Did it come without omens?

The stones under our feet
may as well be fake
and as I look, they are.

Pick-Up at the Dead End Supermarket

Despair is puddling into corners,
jamming automatic doors,
leaking from vents in freezer units.
Persistence is waiting, not so patiently,
to be cleaned up on aisle eight.
You sort through aging passion fruit, some lemons
from the outskirts of a jungle brimming with love.
I'm looking for a not-too-moldy bread of life—
preferably crusty on the outside, soft on the inside,
like me. Let's leave this joint, jump into the car,
race to a meadow.
It's June, after all, and I just wanted to say hi.

Ellijay

Amazing how much the ground can drink—
or perhaps it's already drowned,
body floating belly up—earthfish.
The truck is stuck
in the mud. This is a town
easy to not notice, not find.
I'm definitely here and involuntarily
still—in the place where I grew up.
How the earth sparkles with mica,
a daytime reflection of the night.
Isn't that what this red clay is for—
stopping time, replaying later?
Or possibly early fortune-telling,
drawn with hunks of soft-colored earth.
We were naming the rain puddles after oceans,
naming the transient,
picturing the puddlefish named after stars,
picturing the rainstars named,
picturing us named, intransigent.

Elderly Breasts

They somehow manage
to slip
to the floor
when a woman's not aware
and travel
to her husband. Still
wrinkled, they take
to the new house and flourish,
not flowers,
by any stretch of the imagination,
but pelican beaks full with fish.
Cut open the breast of man
and find live mackerel.
It's worth the effort.

Eating His Dead Wife

It doesn't even seem weird anymore,
eating his dead wife's ashes
in his cereal every morning.
He enjoys being with her every day,
her inside him for a change.
If the cereal is sweetened,
he thinks of her eyes.
Bran reminds him of her navel
and how like a bowl it is.
He doesn't know what will happen
when he runs out of her again.

Silk-Spinner

He is a human spider,
the way he wraps the silk
around anything that will hold it:
the chair he reads in at dusk,
the threads disappearing
in and out of the light.
He winds around tiny trees,
misformed, bottom-heavy
like his late wife.
He is winding her
around the porch posts,
around the light itself and the wind
when it's blowing
and the stillness when it's not.

Burial

When Uncle was buried,
    it was on top of Great-Grandfather
        for the cemetery had long been full on the ground
        floor.
Uncle was able to meet Great-Grandfather
    for the first time since he was seven.
        Uncle was surprised by Great-Grandfather's
        gingham dress,
which, Great-Grandfather explained, was Cousin's.
    Being buried next to each other, they had
        mixed together during their melting period.

They were looking forward to what Uncle would bring.
    Would he ante up a new toe for the ones that were lost?
    (Such is the absent-mindedness of the dead.)
Great-Grandfather/Cousin also needed a belt
    and memories of a colorful bird in a green, green tree.
        They wanted again to see what the eyes see as they
        rot away,
the beautiful distortions of the earth.

The Statue Licker

The obsession started in the Krakow salt mines,
where they encourage guests to lick the art.
He was surprised to find art has many flavors,
like berries in parks at night.
In museums, he became the master of disguise.
Greek statues taste like figs and lemons.
The Renaissance created dishes so complex
he was made famous by their reproduction.
The doctors could not decide whether he died
from starvation or gluttony—the body tasted of rosemary.

Cat

She was only in the corner
of my eye at first, calico
on orange tile, growing
until the whole roof speckled
white and black.
But it is only a cat,
even though she scurries
up the roof so comfortably,
it seems she'll run all the way
to the clouds and be
the first cat in heaven.
Ave Calico, Ave
the tomcat joining her now.
The cats are gathering slowly,
each enjoying the sun,
yawning to let it reach down into
the stomach and radiate back out,
making mooncats, prowling moon,
moon in heat.

Astronomy

My attention is decisively
on the girl outside with the small dog.

She is picking her way through trees,
the leaves patterned on her already-patterned dress.

She moves into the sunlight and her hair becomes the sun.

The dog worships the sun-goddess;
when she sits on a rock, he crawls to her lap.

She gives him freedom, drops the leash
and he, mud-colored, orbits her still.

They are moving again.
The dog is sniffing and the girl circles him.

Astronomy is turned back five hundred years.

Saying Goodbye to the Slugs

A wet fall so there were many,
black and thick like tire strips
crawling to the garage,
collecting gum wrappers and coins
to build a car, one they could propel
into infamy—a Slugmobile gunning for the open road.

The solution to overpopulation was common—
ship a colony to a new land.
We selected Slugquistadores,
built a raft of twigs, leaves, mud,
launched them into the lake,
new kings of the watery road.

I've Never Told Him This

The way his lips crack,
chap like continental plates
always ready to raze
a city—my skin
does that at night.
I walk out of myself
become what he wants,
a fish in the lake.
He has his quirks too—

his fear coming out as a possum.
He doesn't even know
it's going to happen.
(He never thinks
of what will happen.)

Expanding infinitely is a loss of self,
which is why he feeds
on whatever enters the eye.

Undressing with eyes?

I'm curling the skin back—
a way to climb inside.

The Stuffed Dog

Once you have the dog stuffed
you're forced to witness his death again—
the dust settling on the still coat;
the gradual wearing away of skin where
you rest your hand to remember warmth.
This ancient carpet, you used to love,
only sorrow, guilt and disappointment,
a sadness that can never lay down.

Puddle Bird

This bird is splashing in a puddle,
in mid-air, hovering
hummingbird-like
over the street,
bird feet
dangling beneath cloud.
Though it is unclear
what is holding
the puddle up, the puddle
is clearly holding up the bird.
The bird becomes a duck,
and the birds on the ground
who refuse to use
sky-puddles must duck
as they drift by.

The Killed Bug

The bug started decomposing under the bed
giving off the scent of flowers and curry.
Dreams started scurrying
from the bed at odd hours.
Soon clouds crawled out as well,
unlit candles, whole novellas,
heroines dressed in blue,
shimmering like fish scales,
blues of urgency—still the smells!
Finally it seemed the bed had creeped
out from under itself, given birth to itself,
rocked itself to sleep.
It was reborn solid lightning,
so inviting and strange.

The Break Up

The rain is coming only
from the trees and the buildings.
Other things are wrong with this scene.
For instance, it is unclear
if the principals are melting or being formed.
Everything is stopped
and The Uncertainty Principle may mean
that as observers, we can never know what
would have occurred without this being written.
These principals, we furthermore do not know
who was talking between them,
who was it that said the lingering,
"It is over. It was never
to be." This has not reached the other.
The very fact that we are observing this
could change the path forever—
could send it back to the sayer,
who may or may not be strong enough to hear it.
Perhaps it will even come to us.
Though we have never actually met the couple,
I do not want to hear those words fall.

It's Late Autumn and the Few Leaves Left Clinging to the Trees Beg to Be Pulled Off

On TV the B-movie actress
is plucking more from the man's lips than the sound—
she wants to steal the leaf
from his inner-most tree with her tongue.
But her acting skills won't cover it.
She's too preoccupied with the man
from the bar last night who got her drunk,
left her with a wrong number and the check.
She stood in the predictable rain, 4 A.M.,
with more clothes than she wished to be wearing.
So what she's wanting is not only the soul's leaf
but to take the skin as well as the clothes
off the man now in front of her.
In the background, there's a print of Dali's
*As a Child, I Lifted the Skin of the Sea
to Uncover a Dog Sleeping.* She knows
what else is under those waves.
She's scared the hidden earth and all its baggage
will crush the rented set and her thin
life's plot will show.
                    It's too late.
That earth is already there. It was there before.
The Indian mound-builders from set thirty-seven brought it.
Even without ever seeing the film, they know bad acting.

Still

Time is thrown
into fire, smoke
caught in air,
tossed off
as moths, dry
and falling to ground.

You enter my thoughts
as a roach into a kitchen
in a house sleeping,
nestled into ground—

weight pulling down,
flames rising up.

The Empty Mailbox

The mailbox has been empty for days
and in the fertility of August
it has already grown wild.
Vines sprout from its open mouth and a tiny stray dog
jumps to the box and curls into home.
Days pass and a small worm,
living in a puddle at the box's leg,
buds legs and begins to crawl,
evolving into a small species of bird
with the call of late night radio.
The dog survives on the meat of the birds
until they become extinct, and then
follows that road. Fall will come soon
and the forest of the mailbox will become bare.
Perhaps then, your letters will again migrate home.

Nightmare

Sleep was hiding in the corner
afraid of the dark as a nightmare
crossed the sky. There was nothing
I could do to comfort you, love,
eyes docking and unloading
at a pier sunk a hundred years.
Voices were being mined in your head,
the past brought to the surface with black lung.
You were beyond me and slipping,
drowning already,
when the cyclone, strength of demons,
hit the shore.

A Possibility

It may have happened in the years that barked,
years with a tail, made up of days of intestines and fur.
It may have happened like this—
A man walks down a sidewalk.
He thinks of the next day at 3 P.M.
when he's thinking back to walking down the sidewalk
and so he makes an infinite time loop in his mind and thus,
becomes eternal.
In one version of this story, a woman is passing the man.
She has breasts like bursting oranges.
She is not making herself immortal in her thoughts.
She is an artist and is creating a storm.
Even the man is pulled out of his thoughts
long enough to notice the clouds.

The Bird Eats a Building

The bird lands in a puddle,
instantly shattering the reflection of a building,
which she eats in pieces
like a cracker crushed in soup.
She dips her wings into pavement,
throws her head backwards,
gargles a copier before flying away,
leaving the puddle to grow a skyscraper—
like Prometheus developing a new liver each night,
the price for stealing fire.

Walterdon, Scientist

A man is sewing
the head of a lizard
to the body of a rat.
It is a marvelous creature but it is not.
He has spent time
in the Amazon collecting
madness like fruit,
crawling through trees,
a monkey with the cry of a parrot,
a jaguar ambushing water.
He does not know he is not a god
and the world needs this thing.

In Puerto Angel

The wild grandmother
slipped out the window.
It was the kind of day
when anyone who could speak Spanish
could speak nothing else.
The trees were shouting
to each other, "Los besos, los besos."
The children caught in between crawled away.
There was an old woman
handing out candy in the square.
The cobblestones were tense and
looking for crumbs. The sea
waiting to devour the sun.

I Have Other Things on My Mind

This cap keeps me warm enough—
who needs Hell?
Hell is driving this road at night, at Christmas
with the shapes of angels hovering over a small town
waiting to be lit by the torch of a one-hour parade.
Santa will be on the fire truck
waving to the children before rushing to the mall.
He'll get a speeding ticket on the way.
The sheriff will ask, "Where's the fire?"
and get nothing in his stocking.
Too bad, he had asked for a better mousetrap
which only the elves could build.
They came up with the idea after building ten thousand
       talking Mickeys.
They need rubidium, number thirty-seven on the periodic
       table.
But Mrs. Claus already cleaned the table and did the dishes
and tucked all the good elves in bed.
Good thing—rubidium spontaneously combusts the air
and violently decomposes water.
It could do a hell of a job on a mouse.
No mouse will be stirring this Christmas Eve.
The cookie batter will have to wait.
Let them eat cake.
Off with their heads.
Who needs rubidium;
a good guillotine always does the trick.

Cruel Son

He plucked out his mother's right eye
to make these pickles,
boiled it in brine then tossed in the cucumbers.
No—he plucked out his mother's
right eye to make these pickles
then put brine in the darkness
to make her cry;
then fed her a pickle from the batch
so she could see again.

French Recipe

First the bird must be processed through itself,
folded tightly and pushed into beak.
The bird takes several days to digest itself.
After this, it is important to migrate south—
the next step takes the sun and sea.
The bird must sit in a blue chair under a blue umbrella
in a perfect row until browned,
basting itself in the brine of ocean,
then fly to the mountains
to be swallowed by a goat,
who will eat young greens until vomiting.
The bird is now herb-encrusted.
It should be hunted the following season,
filled with mushrooms and small mammals,
cooked over an open fire.
It should be eaten quickly—
you are the next step in earth's meal.

Just a Moment Ago

The clouds aligned so that the trees lost their magnetism.
Birds fell to the ground, sputtering to stay graceful.

A squirrel bounded over the trampoline of earth.
But what has this to do with you?

You must be the stream, for even by yourself, you are plural—
confusing the verbs you pass through.

But you are not the stream, you are the rock in the stream, rocking
        the moss to sleep,
letting the water take you a little at a time like a good seduction.

Or perhaps you are the river sand,
holding the throat of the world.

Snake

The cabin was dark and silent. The old woman
had hair to the floor, braided and snake-like.
The adults talked as adults and we were sent outside.
There was a snake by the creek.

No one remembers this but us,
even though news split out of us like seeds.
No one remembers even the old woman,
her hair reaching the creek, winding back,

a bridge of hair between us.

Traveling

The moment of discovery—
leaving a tunnel or a cloud
to found a new city in the soul.
Is this how you feel when we are alone?
I feel something rushing out of me,
mantis hatching in thousands,
a thousand prayers of Japanese paper,
covering the church.

The prayers have escaped the building as young cannibals,
gaining strength, flying toward the sky.

If I lived on Mir I could repair myself like a strange insect.
I could leave myself and cluster onto my skin.
I could discover your skin again.
I could be islands entering your mouth
like so many huge moths.

The water not as a mirror but a window.
I could enter you and found an empire.

Hiking in Slovenia

We started in a small town
at the foot of a small Alp.
Fingers, gestures, words in no language,
the word "church" in every language,
and the beginning of the trail
quickly turning into nothingness,
a limbo heading straight up.

It seemed more dangerous to go down than up.
Three walking sticks broken; spirit broken;
determination and dirt to hold onto
and then, the sound of small voices.
Whether they were angels to help us or
angels to drive us back into the earth,
they failed. We made it to the top.

The frescoes were primitive
and we headed down not talking,
not knowing the name of the village we began in.
The way down was as hard as the way up.
We were sinking back
into earth that would not accept us, and we were lost.

Lily

You weren't around when the lily bloomed.
It was shocking to see—
the head so much larger than the stalk.
Then a second bloom where none should fit.
When it rained, they each turned from white to yellow.
The sun had grown from a bulb.
The bulb had burst into a soft boiled egg.
The bulb in your lamp bled your absence.

Tonight I Can Write the Saddest Lines

—Neruda

The lake glows just before dark as if throwing
its borrowed light off its shoulders—
a dancer's robe—as if saying,
"Moon, I reject everything
you stand for." As if the moon stands
for anything. How laughable is the moon
as an equal sign.
The moon is an inequality—
"You are less
than something," it says.
Ignore it—grab a beer and the dog,
pull up a lawn chair. The dawn is coming.
Until then, the lake is a black hole.
We will sit at the edge.

The Day the Air Conditioning
Broke in the Wax Museum

It's like Marilyn Monroe's breasts are onions, layers are just falling
    off.
Jimmy Carter is sweating, south Georgia style, and still smiling.
It was never this hot in politics.
Einstein's thoughts are finally tamed and follow the parade down
    his arms.
They sleep on the floor tonight.
In the hall of horrors, the executioners are wondering, "What have
    I done to deserve this?"
and the prisoners are free.
The Amazon tribe, decorating bodies so their souls can't escape, are
    losing.
Every one of them. The souls are flying around the ceiling.
The saints aren't in any better shape but at least they're used to
    suffering.
Saint Catherine thinks this is just another hallucination, watching
    the others melt.
She's trying to interpret it while her brain slips down her throat.
There's a whole Garden of Eden melting into one.
The floor is sticking to my shoes.
I'm taking nirvana with me.

Lemon Breast of the Virgin Mary

Up near the neck,
sticking out from unperforated cloth
like some new miracle,
it's shaped like a small lemon.
Young Jesus reaches for lemonade,
or bites the rind.
Mary does not seem alarmed
at her partial transformation to tree
like a common nymph.
She never seems surprised
to have given birth to an old man.
She does not even seem to notice
the encroaching cross, appearing
at the edge of the painting.
She is the essence of vegetal calm,
unlike her Roman counterparts,
so much pleading to remain a virgin from the gods.

Picking Blueberries

Morning has not gone more than a dozen paces
but the air is already milking us with its heat.
We milk the vines, feel the fruit fall through the hand.
The sound of berries hitting the bucket
speaks the ripeness of the world,
hanging low and heavy,
still and wonderful. I smell like earth.
And Lord, I'm bearing fruit.

The Man is Walking His Bird on a Leash

The leash is attached to a harness
because the bird once pulled so hard,
she tore a hole through the air,
leaving the man with a mess he could only
patch over with his breath, taping the edges
in an awkward manner.
The city council gave him a ticket
for using duct tape on the sky.
And what does the bird think of all this?
She dreams constantly of the other side of sky.

Horse Tracks

What if there was a place
in one of those ancient grooved roads

where the horses had gone mad
so often you had no choice

but to follow their tracks, to go mad too.
And what if that place were in the atmosphere,

following weather patterns, or a woman,
about to walk through the door.

Outside the Moon

Outside the moon
is erased
by a cloud—
it is being
formed backwards.

Inside, the light
is not calm,
but blown
around the room
by the fan,
held hostage in
corners by spiders.

The mountains are rotting
away with the moon.
Only the tops
are present now.
They are slowly sinking.

I know this bread
is my own sadness,
but I eat it
and am still hungry.

The Bird as a Painting

This bird is part of the window—caught in mid-flight,
crystallized like rock candy.
The tree behind her is also false,
reduced to two dimensions by a calloused eye.
A dog walks into the scene,
becoming trapped as well. The entire world
has been condensed to this pane of contentious glass.
Even a stone has no depth—
the stone, the end of days.

Home Sick

I was just calling to tell you
my socks don't match today,
the coffee maker's brewing melancholy,
and it's cold here.

I was just calling to tell you
the Turks conquered Europe with tulips.
I'm sending you some next week.

I was just calling to tell you
longing looked in my window while I slept.
This morning I cleaned his face print from the glass.

I was just calling to tell you
when all my being took flight,
a thousand moths thought of you.

Saying Goodbye to a Friend

Not needing a fire but starting one
because we already had the wood.
The smoke becoming women,
then a deep fog with men disappearing
into the ground.
The sound of low country music,
behind that the sound of crickets.
The driver tipsy,
backing into cholla,
a piece in your friend's leg,
then rolling around,
poltergeist in the truck bed.
Out of the headlights,
you shrink
into the lit end of your cigarette.

About the Author

Danielle Hanson holds an MFA from Arizona State University and an undergraduate degree from the University of Tennessee at Chattanooga. She is Poetry Editor of Doubleback Books, on the editorial staff for *Loose Change Magazine* and is a former poetry editor for *Hayden's Ferry Review*. Her poetry has appeared in over 50 journals and anthologies, has been nominated for Pushcart and Best of the Net awards, and has received the Vi Gale Award from *Hubbub*. She works as a marketing executive for AT&T Entertainment Group.

Our Mission

The mission of Brick Road Poetry Press is to publish and promote poetry that entertains, amuses, edifies, and surprises a wide audience of appreciative readers. We are not qualified to judge who deserves to be published, so we concentrate on publishing what we enjoy. Our preference is for poetry geared toward dramatizing the human experience in language rich with sensory image and metaphor, recognizing that poetry can be, at one and the same time, both familiar as the perspiration of daily labor and as outrageous as a carnival sideshow.

BRICK ROAD
POETRY PRESS

Also Available from Brick Road Poetry Press
www.brickroadpoetrypress.com

Bad Behavior by Michael Steffen

Tracing the Lines by Susanna Lang

Rising to the Rim by Carol Tyx

Treading Water with God by Veronica Badowski

Rich Man's Son by Ron Self

Just Drive by Robert Cooperman

The Alp at the End of My Street by Gary Leising

The Word in Edgewise by Sean M. Conrey

Household Inventory by Connie Jordan Green

Practice by Richard M. Berlin

A Meal Like That by Albert Garcia

Cracker Sonnets by Amy Wright

Things Seen by Joseph Stanton

Battle Sleep by Shannon Tate Jonas

Lauren Bacall Shares a Limousine by Susan J. Erickson

Also Available from Brick Road Poetry Press

www.brickroadpoetrypress.com

Dancing on the Rim by Clela Reed

Possible Crocodiles by Barry Marks

Pain Diary by Joseph D. Reich

Otherness by M. Ayodele Heath

Drunken Robins by David Oates

Damnatio Memoriae by Michael Meyerhofer

Lotus Buffet by Rupert Fike

The Melancholy MBA by Richard Donnelly

Two-Star General by Grey Held

Chosen by Toni Thomas

Etch and Blur by Jamie Thomas

Water-Rites by Ann E. Michael

About the Prize

The Brick Road Poetry Prize, established in 2010, is awarded annually for the best book-length poetry manuscript. Entries are accepted August 1st through November 1st. The winner receives $1000 and publication. For details on our preferences and the complete submission guidelines, please visit our website at www.brickroadpoetrypress.com.